YOU ARE YOUR FINANCES

HONORABLE MENCHAN MEDIA

#JUSTLOVEMINISTRY 2018

Angelia Vernon Menchan

904 303 2679

acvermen@yahoo.com

1

ARE YOU EATING YOUR FINANCIAL SECURITY?

I'm sure you're staring at me, wondering what does that mean. Well, I am going to tell you.

If you feel it is necessary to eat most meals out with reasoning such as, it's just me at home; you're likely eating your financial security. Here is a breakdown of what that means, at bare minimum.

Breakfast:

Average fast food sandwich with coffee: $4.99 or $25.00 weekly at 5 Days.

Lunch:

Average lunch out with beverage: $7.99 or $40.00 weekly at 5 Days.

Dinner or Supper:

Average takeout meal: $10.00 or $50.00 weekly at 5 Days.

That's $115.00 for meals out weekly. Even if only cutting out dinner that's $50.00 for savings or $2600 dollars annually. Even if you prepare meals at home for dinner at half that price that is $1300.00 saved annually and you still get two meals out per day.

One rotisserie chicken from Sam's Club is $5.00 and about four servings for the average person and it's already cooked. Throw in one sweet potato, a pound of green beans and a cabbage and for $8.00 you have four meals. That is less one dinner, two breakfasts or one lunch out. On the next pages I need you to track all meals out by cost.

Monday

Breakfast_____

Lunch_____

Dinner_____

Snacks including soda and bottled
water_____

Tuesday

Breakfast_____

Lunch_____

Dinner_____

Snacks including soda and bottled
water_____

Wednesday

Breakfast_____

Lunch_____

Dinner_____

Snacks including soda and bottled
water_____

Thursday

Breakfast_____

Lunch_____

Dinner_____

Snacks including soda and bottled
water_____

Friday

Breakfast_____

Lunch_____

Dinner_____

Snacks including soda and bottled
water_____

I am not including Saturday and Sundays. All
plans need days with treats. Once you have
completed the first week, plan a grocery list for
week two and only purchase what you need for
all meals or the meal or meals out you plan to
eliminate. At the end of week two compare
expenses. If you do not already have a savings
account, start one and accrue your savings
rather than eating them.

CAN YOU AFFORD TO LOOK THAT FLY?

This is the area where I step on my own toes. I love dresses, handbags and red lipstick and I have an excess of all. When I travel I purchase bags of the country or venue. I also donate to causes where a bag is included. I also purchase bags as if... I don't have any. The same is true with dresses... often I excuse it by saying I'm supporting this one or that one who sells dresses or it's 40 percent off. Ummm. My biggest excuse is I have savings and investments so what's the big deal. The big deal is I wear them once or twice. I could invest more or donate to causes that need me.

We all want to dress well and look nice but not at the expense of owning a home, investing, saving for higher education or to be able to retire one day.

Even if the clothing is from reduced priced stores such as TJMAXX, ROSS or even Wal-mart, if we have nine black dresses we do not need another. What we need to do is address what we are trying to fill by owning so much stuff... often that buying fills a need being unmet in other ways. Do we shop because we are lonely, sad, angry or disappointed and figure if nothing else, I can look good and have people applaud me? On the next pages I need you to be completely honest about your shopping habits and how getting new things make you feel, even when you know purchasing it will leave you short of funds.

I also need you to list things you would and could do with money you save from NOT shopping for things you already own.

List shopping habits and why... how it makes you feel during and after. It is truth telling time.

_____

_____

_____

_____

_____

_____

_____

What would you do with the proceeds if you didn't shop your feelings? BE very expansive and honest.

_____

_____

_____

_____

_____

_____

_____

_____

_____

WAYS TO PAY OFF BILLS EARLY!

Do you have a mortgage?

If you answered yes, you can very easily make one extra payment per month, reducing your thirty year mortgage by years. How? I'm glad you asked.

Talk to your lender and set up twice monthly payments. If your mortgage is 1000 dollars pay 500 dollars twice monthly, on say the 2nd and 16th or any two week interval. This translates to 26 payments or 13 payments annually. There are 52 weeks per year and if you pay every other week that's thirteen weeks. Those payments shave months off the life of your loan.

Do You Have Charge Cards?

Of course you do...

If trying to eliminate debt, stop using them except by necessity. We all need them to travel, make reservations, etc. but many times we use them on frivolities. It makes no sense to pay interest on McDonald's fries no matter how tasty they are.

Also minimum payments will never rid you of credit card debt. Increase your payments and control your spending. If it's perishable such as food, liquor et al stop using credit unless you are using your credit card to accrue miles or rewards and pay them off monthly.

Otherwise for every 100 dollars you pay most is going to interest. I'm telling you what I know. We were once almost 30,000 in credit card debt and other than furniture and paying for my mom's funeral it was all frivolous spending. We buckled down, agreed to stop using unless emergencies and doubled our payments and in less than three years we were debt free.

Debt free allows us to do things we love and provides for what we need.

A great way to save is as soon as you pay off a bill turn that money immediately into an account, you didn't have it for the length of the car therefore you can afford to save it.

(I moved from Kentucky to Florida to live with my family and my husband was deployed in Turkey... we had paid off his car but the bank was still taking out the allotment... I contacted the bank and had them roll over monthly to our savings. When he returned, we were able to pay for a new car.)

If you receive a raise at work, immediately before you receive it, place in your savings, DO NOT MAKE PLANS to spend it before you get it.

Another thing is if you receive a bonus, spend some on you, you have earned it but earmark a percentage for savings.

Utilize Your Skills

As a teen I started several businesses. The first was candied apples. I made yellow, green and purple ones giving me a specialty item. I also sold for a nickel cheaper...

In high school I wrote book reports and term papers for a fee. I read the books and did the research and they earned the grade. I also tutored other students...

Can you cook or bake? You can sell food.

Can you clean well? You can clean offices and homes.

Do you enjoy children or the elderly? You can be a caregiver.

Can you drive? Drive for Uber or one of the other taxi-like services.

Can you type, proofread or edit? Authors, publishers and others pay for these services.

This is a small list of things we can do to earn streams of income to add to our bottom line.

In all these things don't forget to give. A hand open in giving is never empty. God gives to us manifold for what we give to others. I'm a witness with a testimony.

This is going to seem small but small savings buy things. In my family we throw change in containers, leaving it there for months, sometimes years. When we were leaving Oklahoma to move to Florida we had more than $500.00 in change. We used that money to pay for hotels, gas and food as we drove across country...

Please ask questions about finances and make notes of what I offer and others share. We can be financially healthy together.

_____

_____

_____

_____

_____

_____

_____

_____

_____

_____

www.ingramcontent.com/pod-product-compliance
Lightning Source LLC
Chambersburg PA
CBHW071200220526
45468CB00003B/1093